KINDRED

2018 Savant Poetry Anthology

Edited by Doc Krinberg

Savant Books and Publications
Honolulu, HI, USA
2018

Published in the USA by Savant Books and Publications
2630 Kapiolani Blvd #1601
Honolulu, HI 96826
http://www.savantbooksandpublications.com

Printed in the USA

Edited by Doc Krinberg
Cover by Daniel S. Janik
Cover Image "Locks" by laurahatcherphotography.com with permission

13 digit ISBN: 9780999463307

First Edition: June 2018
Library of Congress Control Number: 2018949274

Dedication

This collection is dedicated to those who still report from those front lines of humanity on our condition.

Acknowledgements

A special thanks to Laura Hatcher for her offer of the love-lock photo taken high above Golden Bate Bridge.

The locks, together in perpetuity against time, elements, the touch of visitors held a special meaning for the title. Kindred souls, spirits, and strangers, we all hang in the balance holding our own against life.

Table of Contents

(in order of appearance)

Forward

kindred | ˈkindrəd | noun [treated as plural] one's family and relations. • relationship by blood: ties of kindred. adjective [attributive] similar in kind; related: books on kindred subjects.

We may not all be bound by blood, but there is a profound DNA that binds our experiences and personal trajectories, pushing up inside of us and when harnessed and written, spells how much we are the same; love, desire, plans, failures. The universal needs of love and spiritual peace come thru in Kindred as well as the tragic accidents that occur in even the most balanced relationships rendering us lost in that wilderness of pain that is sometimes singular to the human condition.

One need not be bound by genes to be a kindred soul to one who while living across the globe suffers the same pain, exalts in the same pleasure, or observes both coolly from afar to see we are so close.

Poetry is that universal bridge.

Dorothy Winslow Wright is a multi-award-winning, internationally published author. Her poetry has appeared in numerous literary anthologies and magazines, including *Blue Unicorn, Mature Living, Poet, The Foralist, Time of Singing* and the *Atlantic Advocate.* She is an active member of the National League of American PEN Women Honolulu Branch, currently living in Honolulu, Hawaii, USA.

Notable prose contributions include:
THE BOOK GROUP BOOK by Ellen Slezak (Ed) (Chicago Review Press 1993)

Office Black and Dusty Pink

by Dorothy Winslow Wright

I see my mother stepping from the bus,
slender ankles in lisle stockings, tiny feet
in trim black shoes. I waited every day
at five-fifteen, two blocks from home.

I wore my roller skates. Skimmed along the
smooth, slick asphalt. Smiled when I caught
her eye. At home she changed from office
black to dusty pink and became my mother
again. In mellow light, I wrote on a
blue-lined pad, my little sister sprawled
on the floor beside me. Mother never asked
about homework; that was our concern.

Her black dress hung on the bathroom door,
the steam from the tub easing out the wrinkles.
Always the same black dress. There was no
money for a new one. But we had new shoes
when we needed them—brown and practical
and a size too big. I would stretch my skates
to fit the shoes with my chunky, silver key.

We seldom spoke of Dad. When he came to
take us to the park on Saturdays, how glorious
it was. Golden castles rose into the air—tall,
piercing the sky! Fairies danced and diamonds

tipped the meadow grass. Such dreams we wove
of what would be when his "ship came in"
but I knew his ship would never come to port.

When he left, the diamonds dimmed and the
fairies drifted off. In the quiet evening, my
mother and I listened to the radio. I sat on
the floor beside her chair, my head on her dusty
pink lap learning of love through her fingertips.

Water Lilies

by Dorothy Winslow Wright

The rowboat lay on a curve of sand as if
awaiting me, the nine year old who yearned
to see the water lilies before returning
home—if there was such a place. I wasn't sure.

No one heard me leave. No one dreamed
a spindly city kid not known for physical
prowess would consider such a venture.
They didn't know the lure of water lilies
to a child unused to quiet country ponds.

I rowed among the lily pads, their graceful
stems parting for my splendid craft—

I, a sylvan princess, gliding through
my water garden surveying my realm to lilting
birdsong chorus. Wavelets lapped the boat
in contrapuntal harmony. Star-like
flowers flaunting their exquisite dress in the seductive
spell of a pond at early dawn. Pale green
buds flashed delicate signs of promise the way
a prepubescent girl feels the gentle stirrings
of something changing within her body.

I drifted, trying to understand the changes
underway—my father gone, my brother
going with him. We would be on our own, my mother, sister
and I. We would live somewhere in Boston, a city new to me.
With misty eyes, I rowed to shore. Returned
to the cottage that housed me that one brief week. Sat
on the steps breathing in the pine scented air.
I might forget the cottage, but not the woods,
the quiet pond and the peaceful water lilies.

Genetic Strings

by Dorothy Winslow Wright

"Children begin by loving their parents. As they grow older, they judge them; sometimes they even forgive them." - Oscar Wilde

Parental bodies blend when love songs
fill the quiet hours, their romance
caught in embryo, their beloved child,
inheritor of two genetic strains, a weave of both.

A joy. A love. Bounced on knees, raised
with daddy's hugs and mummy's kisses.
raised between shouts and weepy make-up
scenes of feisty parents still connected.

She doesn't like the fights, but knows
they will kiss and forgive as they have
before. Closes her eyes to her mother's
tears, her ears to her fathers excuses.

When divorce creeps in, she learns to
wear a mask, to spout expected loyalties,
but the severing---how painful it is,
the genetic strings too tightly knit to loosen.

Wollaston Beach

by Dorothy Winslow Wright

He had a can of tuna in the car, a loaf
of bread, his smile as wide as summer.
"A picnic," Dad said. We were off to

the beach, my brother, sister and I.

Few were the times we saw each other.
Sam lived with dad, we girls with mum.
Too old to dress in cars, we wore our
bathing suits beneath our clothes.

Sam was sixteen, and tall. Brown hair
that waved like mine, though mine was red.
Ann's hair was blonde and straight as grass,
but our eyes were all the same. Hazel.

Hazel touched with unexpected shyness
as we strived for easy camaraderie. Would
it come? None of us were sure as we tiptoed
into conversation. Did Sam like girls?

He might. I saw him blush when we doffed
our shirts. We were girls with shapes he
hadn't seen on us before. We raced him to
the water. Shivered in the south shore waves.

Lips blue, we trembled under towels, but when
our father spread the bread with tuna, we all
dug in, the shyness gone as dripping fish oil
greased our chins, the giggles taking over.

The Charmer

by Dorothy Winslow Wright

A flat straw boater dipped below his eyes
In pre-depression style
my father, an elegant man
accustomed to the finest things (black ties
and tails, and canted wine) ignored
the threadbare flannels skimming his lanky thighs.

He strode through Boston's Public Garden, hat
in place, fingers grazing brim,
smiling at the ladies, an aristocrat
caught in dappled sunlight,
his breezy air convincing
none but me, who wouldn't face the facts.

He was my Father Prince;
divorced, debonair,
his slender fingers stained with nicotine,
a sophisticated man
who made an unsure duckling feel a queen
who took me to lunch the day I turned thirteen.

Daniel S. Janik is a physician, educator, environmentalist, linguist, author, poet photographer and videographer with over seventy published works across numerous genres and a variety of pen names. A multi-award-winning poet, he has contributed to numerous poetry books and anthologies, and was recognized as a 2007 Poet of the Year. He is the recipient of a New Millennium Writer's Award, Eric Hoffer Award, Neurobiological Learning Society Award, London and Amsterdam Book Festival Awards, several Pacific Rim Book Festival Award, and both LA and Hollywood Book Festival Awards.

Notable works poetic works include:
FOOTPRINTS, SMILES AND LITTLE WHITE LIES by Daniel S. Janik (Savant 2008)
THE ILLUSTRATED MIDDLE EARTH by Daniel S. Janik (Savant 2008)
LAST AND FINAL HARVEST by Daniel S. Janik (Savant 2008).

Notable prose works include:
A WHALE'S TALE by Daniel S. Janik (Savant 2009)
THE TURTLE DANCES by Daniel S. Janik (Savant 2013)
UNLOCK THE GENIUS WITHIN by Daniel S. Janik (Rowman and Littlefied 2005)
KINGSLEY & I by Gary Martine (MLR Press 2008)
KINGSLEY & I TOGETHER by Gary Martine (MLR Press, 2009)
KINGSLEY & I RELOADED by Gary Martine (Createspace 2012)
TOTAL MELTDOWN by Raymond Gaynor and William Maltese (Borgo/Wildside 2009)
QUANTUM DEATH by A. G. Hayes with Raymond Gaynor (Savant 2016).

Kehei Beach

by Daniel S. Janik

I wish
The silvered waves of time
To fit into my daily rhyme;

I ask
The curls of sunlit white,
To enter dreams I want tonight.

I call
Water creatures each to bind,
The expectations in my mind.

Ocean, grasses, rocks and sea,
I command you yield to me!

Then, in desperation

I curse
The stark and cloudless sky,
For never reasons, only whys.

Another Night

by Daniel S. Janik

Another Toastum pop-up night,
the man in striped slacks
mused
as rain streaked eyes everywhere about him
painfully lowered their window shades.

The fog yawned,
Disinterested,
condensed and fell
upon his felt-covered shoulders.

Another thought soon
precipitated
slowly,
heavily,
syrup sticky,
flowing down his soaked clothes
and into the sewers.

Tonight,
Just like the one before,
dims the street lamps
all about
Like faulty Christmas lights,
they desperately try to flicker
one more time

before being packed away another year.

Lenin's Tomb

by Daniel S. Janik

Tucked somewhere deep in the shadows of Red Square
Lies a grey concrete building
Protecting a grey concrete man
while on the cobblestones outside
the spirit of Mother Russia
files past
weeping
not for him
but for her newest children.

Beaten,
sad,
alone,
mad,
the grey concrete man
lies
alone,
hands fisted
very much afraid
of the children

filing one by one about him,
his own childhood stolen
long ago.

Ask:
"Who am I?"
"Where are the parents from which I sprang?"
"Where are the mother's arms
that promised to hold me
when I hurt so much inside?"

The darkness will reply:
"You are yourself, nothing more, nothing less."
"You came from yourself."
"You must be there for yourself,
bitter man-child,
when you hurt so much inside."

There is no one left
to help anymore.
Feel,
let live,
let go,
forgive.
Take solace then,
reaching out a ghostly hand
to grasp the wrist of the next passer-by,
in doing so,
passing on
if evanescently so,

the secret dance
that all shuffle by in search of.

Gary "Doc" Krinberg was raised in California where he had a significant amount of dead end jobs to include hot pretzel salesman, strip club barker, parking lot valet, garage attendant and junkyard truck driver before embarking on a career in the US Navy that afforded him significant travel and exposure to many different cultures. Post navy, he pursued graduate and terminal degrees while teaching in various institutions in Japan, Hawaii and mainland America while helping to raise three sons and currently resides in Alexandria, Virginia, where he works at educational consulting, writing and editing poetry. Doc is published in other Savant poetry anthologies to include Lost Tower, UK.

Notable prose contributions include:
POLONIO PASS (Aignos 2014)

THE DEEP SLUMBER OF DOGS (Aignos 2016)

THE WINTER SPIDER (Aignos 2018)

Rain Light

by Doc Krinberg

Prone, vulnerable

Cold in my room
rugs, floor heater,
solace wrapped in a blanket

Drab rain, beading my window

Turning my back to
the grayness upon me
Light without warmth

Becoming skeletal

Adjusting in bed
my back still cold
holding muted rainlight

Mosaics running on glass

Now posturing naked like Frida,
sadly lacking the warmth
of her sensuality

Instead, a mottled corpse

Arching back, a stretching cat
exposed to your eyes
Less than perfect

For an Aging Lothario

by Doc Krinberg

Eye contact at Picabia,
a Monet made you turn smile, but
Klee and Chagall had me winded
Eye tag again as a brown skinned
Gauguin saw me pass Suerat
to a park people rarely know as a
Klimt; your hair caught a nova
as you whirled, the game run, and I
missed a Starry Night, vain pursuit
Moving stairs, now below Wyeth fields
stark Hopper just a memory for this older man
inside my overcoat, between harsh realism and
the unconnected points and colors of youth, but
still chasing the dream.
Coruscate hair and Cheshire smile.

Stacey Lorinn Joy is a second generation native of Los Angeles, California. She has been teaching for 32 years and is recognized as a National Board Certified Teacher and a Los Angeles County Teacher of the Year. She loves poetry, the ocean, and her family.

Notable poetic works include:
NAKED REFLECTIONS: SHAMELESSLY SENSUAL POETRY by Stacey Lorinn Joy (Createspace, 2013)

Rising

by Stacey Lorinn Joy

Breast-fed
Bottle-weaned
Nurtured infantile marriage
Cradled
Coddled
Wedded skin
That I thought was immortal
But fragile translucent veils
Covered a skeleton
Decayed by deceit
I couldn't feed
What was already dead
Ashes buried in
Graveyards of hope.

3:17 a.m.
I listened
To murmurings of joint property
In disrepair
Conjoined parts disjointing
Burning wide-awake
Without air in my fiery nest
Secret cries
Imploding in drawers
Let me fall
Let me crumble

Let me disintegrate.
To the sounds of dawn's solitude
I rocked myself
Back to life
Rising from my blistering heart
Spiritual holes closed
Repurposed faith
Ascending above
The smoky rubbish
Never to return
To the ground

HOLES
by Stacey Lorinn Joy

Women friends
Soul sisters
Ever wonder
Who paves
The path
We cross
Leading us
Various places
Shopping and
Eating and

Kindred

Walking or
Jogging or
Laughing after
Yoga because
Sometimes we
Can’t bend?

Women friends
Soul sisters
Ever wonder
Why we
Don’t take
Advice and
We defend
Broken men
Who drill
Holes into
Our skin
Ripping apart
Smiles that
Never mend?

Women friends
Soul sisters
Ever wonder
How we
Listen with
Our hearts
But the
Holes won't

Hold truth
So we
Scatter it
Like crumbs?

Women friends
Soul sisters
Keep pouring
Your love
Giving encouragement
Sharing stories
And filling
Our holes
Because somewhere
In between
Us eternal
Life flows.

Letting Go

by Stacey Lorinn Joy

When I was seven
I burned bugs with
A magnifying glass

And the sun
I also marveled
At the trillions of
Ants traveling from our
Swimming pool borders
To refuge in the distant grass.
Some carried eggs on their heads
Others scurried in the wrong direction
I wondered if there were some final
Destination of relief
Or were they rushing
To go nowhere.

When I was 51
I destroyed pictures
from a photo album
with scissors and salty tears.
I also smiled at faded snapshots
Of my mother holding my babies
So I could take a nap
From working three jobs.
I wondered if she knew
I couldn't carry all those loads
For a lifetime.
She never had the chance
To see me let go.

Mr. **Bipul Banerjee** is a sales and marketing leader by profession with an MBA and PhD in marketing. Popularly known as"Dusk" in literary circles, he writes poetry for the passion of expression inspired by the emotions he comes across in day-to-day life. He has three research publications, two book chapters and fifteen international and national poetry publications.

THE RAIN BALCONY

by Dusk

Pitter Patter knocks on the French window,
Beckons my soul to free myself
From the jungles of steel
Tar roads also give out petrichor
Concrete loaded trees
Now breathe fresh
Greener than ever
Wink at me with shiny leaves
Artificial air conditioning
Stands no chance
Against the gush;
Moisture of the first rain
Body and soul we rush to
Respond
Pause at the rain balcony
As the drops pick up pace
The quantum of drizzles
Kiss my parched face
The face, which fights daily with
Urban dual standards
The face that is forced to chin up
To adversities and move on
Motherly drizzles
Comfort the tanned skin
That has resisted the heats of change
Arms outstretched

I expose my nude soul
Allowing the greed breeding room
On nature's uncanny nutrition
Old scars and recent wounds
All in joy
For the pouring rains
Now soothe
The wounded
The exposed
The neglected
Exuded inflictions
Washed and cleansed
Disconnect reconnected
My body and soul
Reunite…

Anna Banasiak is a poet and literary critic with interests in art and psychology.

Notable poetic contributions include:
"Varanasi" in FLYING BETWEEN WORDS - Contemporary Writers of Poland (Lulu 2015)

The Dancer

by Anna Banasiak

a drop of water
unique in cosmos
in the changing river of time
passing like a single life
I'm only a shadow
dancing in the emptiness

The art of flying

by Anna Banasiak

Sunrise
stops the essence of existence
ducks immersed in silence
fly free like flames
they dive
stagger sacred circles
my soul
spreads its wings
flying between two worlds
happy upon a moment
brightened by a light
approaches infinity

Masquerade

by Anna Banasiak

I'm leaving my body
the costumes are borrowed
from the changing room of life
my face belongs to a foreign person
for the moment
someone's invisible hand
removes my life
as a used prop
I'm leaving
to start playing
in the new mask

Jana Gartung grew up in a small village in Germany. She attended a Steiner School in Braunschweig where she completed her A-levels in 2016. After that she went to the UK to volunteer in a care home for people with learning disabilities.

TO BE HURT

by Jana Gartung

And always I'm thinking:
I would like to be different.
I would like to be strong.
I would like to have another answer on the question where I'm from.

And I was standing here so often already.
Was hoping for the next step,
But always I'm coming back.

There are so many dreams to live.
So many empty pages to fill.
But still I'm afraid.
Afraid of the loneliness.
Afraid of letting go.
To make the next step
And again be alone.

But every ending is the beginning of something new.
And it is up to you what you wanna be.
Just keep on going.
There is no need for that fear.
It's gonna be alright.
Don't fear the future.
Life can't be always straight
And it's good that it's not,

Enjoy what you have got.
The end's gonna come,
So let's stay strong.

And every end is the beginning of something new.
Life won't stop, because you're not ready yet to come,
It goes on.

And I go out into the world
To find that place within myself
And I aim for places far away
To discover that place wich is always the closest to me.

The view ahead,
Without the thought back.
There isn't just nothing to loose,
There is yet a lot to gain.
You can only loose what isn't you.

Yes, there's gonna be pain,
But there won't be a rainbow without rain.

Go on then, life,
Show me what you can.
Disappoint me again and again,
That I can grow with it.
Hit me again and again,
That I can get stronger out of it.

I don't know what the next destination might be.

There are so many places to see.
No stagnation in sight,
Just the stream of air in my face.

And who knows where I'll be gone,
Maybe in the end I will get strong.
Maybe I will arrive a place which I can call home.
I might not be the strongest
And I might seem weak to you,
But you never know how it will be,
In a few years you might look up to me.

And I go out into the world
To find that place within myself
And I aim for places far away
To discover that place which is always the closest to me.

Questions in the Summer Air

by Jana Gartung

And the moon shines on the silver sea.
The wind plays in the willow tree.
Heavy thoughts pulling me down.
Thoughts made out of sorrow and doubt.
And dropping sadness.

Heavy and thick.
A melancholic loneliness.

And I was standing here so often.
Was hoping of the next step.
But always I'm coming back.
And I'm asking myself when,
when and where will I arrive.

When are we having our happy end?
When am I getting strong?
When am I feeling alright with the questions where I'm from?
So many questions are blowing in the summer air.

And the moon shines on the silver sea.
The wind plays in the willow trees.
And questions are blowing in the summer air.
And I'm wondering:
When are we grown up?
When do I stop dreaming about the one I would like to be?
When can I see that I could already start to be?

But I never thought it is so difficult to get there.
Sp many managed this already,
but for me this burden is just too heavy.
Too many sorrows and fears and fantasies.
Too many worries and doubts and utopian dreams.

Often I'm thinking:
Please wake me up when it’s all over .

When I'm wiser and I'm older.

And questions are blowing in the summer air.
And I'm wondering if we ever reach our aim.
When are these feelings coming to an end?
When do we settle in ourselves?

Maybe it's this age.
You wish to break free of the cage.
Everything is changing.
You are just searching.

Maybe it's this age.
No one seems to be like me.
And no one is feeling that lonely.
But maybe it's really this age.
Maybe this feeling will go away.
Maybe we will find our way.

And I'm watching the moon on the silver sea.
The wind plays in the willow tree.
And I think I can reach the other side,
if I just believe in me.

And questions are blowing in the summer air.
But it is not that painful anymore.
It is something I can bear.
Because now I know.
A question mark is just a twisted exclamation point.

Hongri Yuan, born in China in 1962, is a poet and philosopher interested particularly in creation. Representative works include "Platinum City," "Gold City," "Golden Paradise," "Gold Sun" and "Golden Giant." His poetry has been published in the USA, UK, India, New Zealand, Canada and Nigeria.

THE GARDEN OF THE SOUL

by Hongri Yuan
Translated by Yuanbing Zhang

I beat the world with the sword of nothingness
I have no rivals again
Even the time and the destinies.
So I have a quiet, lonely garden,
the garden of the soul
in which the gods are playing.

THE KINGDOM OF GOLD

by Hongri Yuan
Translated by Yuanbing Zhang

I pulled out of the giant stone
an ancient sword,
its light makes the sun seem dim.
Makes the ancient earth
be transparent and fragrant
as suddenly the purported kingdom of gold.

My Sword is in the Palace Above the Sun

by Hongri Yuan
Translated by Yuanbing Zhang

My sword is in the palace above the sun
My sword is a giant dragon
My sword sometimes flies over the world
In the night of dark iron which the demons are pursuing pleasure
To pierce the head of the giant python to change it into beauty
-----

Smile Is Like the Lotus

by Hongri Yuan
Translated by Yuanbing Zhang

I am sitting in the divine temple of death and my smile is like the lotus
The night runs away and the universe is my garden of light
The quanta outside the sky is my palace of soul in heaven.
Where are prehistoric illustrious scriptures of mine,
and the golden poem created by the giants,
Telling me that the rising, huge city in the future on earth,
will come from the gods' picture scroll of billions of years ago...

As Sweet as the Light of Stars

by Hongri Yuan
Translated by Yuanbing Zhang

The breeze of my finger
Flicked away your earth
You are as transparent as the bead
As sweet as the starlight
The scroll of billions of years
Waking up in your memory.

Cigeng Zhang from China is a freelance translator. She began writing English poems in 2012. Her poems Calla Lily, The Night of Love, Who Do I Meet, Game, and Fish were included in Shadow and Light - 2017 Savant Poetry Anthology. Her bilingual poetry collection ROUGE IN THE WATER was published in China in 2017.

Notable poetic contributions include:
"Drunk Smile" in THE POETIC BOND III edited by Trevor Maynard (Createspace, 2013)

"What Was Left" in THE POETIC BOND IV edited by Trevor Maynard (Createspace, 2014)

"Still for You/ At 8 O'clock/ The Moon, The Poet" in THE POETIC BOND V edited by Trevor Maynard (Createspace 2015)

"Special Reunion/ Hey, Starling/ Wa Lan/ One-Line Tide" in THE POETIC BOND VI edited by Trevor Maynard (Createspace 2016)

"Calla Lily/ The Night of Love/ Who Do I Meet/ Game/ Fish" in SHADOW AND LIGHT - 2017 Savant Poetry Anthology, Helen Davis (ed)

Twin Lotus Flowers

by Cigeng Zhang

Entangled
like twin lotuses
on one stalk
No need of soil
Nor fertilizer

Rich essence
condensed in the roots
nourishes the core
of those twin hearts
It's life and beats solid

Souvenir

by Cigeng Zhang

I bought myself twenty bookmarks
imprinted with Van Gogh paintings
I put a bookmark in one of my favorite books;
'Number the Stars'

My face pressed to the sky in the page
Seeing amazingly, the moon was a poppy!
The color of the dark purple dyed his eyes
Sorrow and inflexible

Millstone

by Cigeng Zhang

Millstone and well
No dog

Wasteland and I
No bard

Dim grey sky
Eyes open

Moonrise
Pushing the millstone, turn

Broken Bridge

by Cigeng Zhang

September is a watershed
Your daytime gets longer
Mine is shorter
Cloud is a broken bridge
Your shore withdraws
Mine tilts

Butterfly looks an avatar

Your love is my illusion
Is my heart still your moon?

Heidi Willson is an English, French, and photography teacher in Rockford, Illinois. She loves writing haiku and senryu poetry forms. In her free time she enjoys hikes in nature and dabbling in photography.

Notable poetic contributions include:
"Prometheus" in GREEK FIRE (Createspace 2015)

"Doggie Dreams" in THE TAIL WAGGED ON (Createspace 2015)

"Peony" in THE POETRY OF FLOWERS (Createspace 2016)

Sight

by Heidi Willson

Midnight pitch black sky
eyes stare into nothingness
begin seeing light
solitary star twinkles
companion in darkest night

Linger

by Heidi Willson

Memory captured
in the fabrics of her soul
never forget how it felt
to feel so whole and complete
infinity lingering

In Between Realms

by Heidi Willson

Lines border heaven;
gray takes up most of earths sky.

Bottom of sky blue,
clear cut borders are painted;
artistic angels drew line.
Some people come close
to entering a sky blue realm
But decide on gray
Paradise isn't perfect
if one's loved ones aren't present.

Kaethe Kauffman (aka Cate Burns) has her Ph.D. in Art History and is an Associate Professor of Art. She has taught at the University of California, Irvine and at Chaminade University in Honolulu among other universities. She has innovated inter-disciplinary team-taught courses in art and writing, and art and psychology.

Notable prose contributions include:
LIBIDO TSUNAMI: Awash with the Droll in Life by Cate Burns (Savant 2016)

Ankle Accolade

by Kaethe Kauffman

Tons of marble teeter on nearly crumbling ankles.
After six hundred years of valiant balancing,
Michelangelo's *David* may begin to wobble,
so scientists say.
Victorious David reminds me,
I owe *my* creaking ankles homage.

They have given me decades of ecstatic jumping,
High skipping,
Dances from tap to hula,
Meandering hikes,
Deep swims,
Long runs,
Leaps off cliffs into heaving oceans.

Now, after seventy winters, simple walks
and occasional twisted yoga positions
stretch my bony knobs askew.

I stand on one leg in Tree Pose,
Left leg straight, but wavering in the
attempt to hold me up.
My right ankle sharply bends to rest on my right thigh.

Sole upright, so I can gaze at it.
Tendons and ligaments bunch,

but I feel free.

The bottom of my foot,
resembles small curved hills in a landscape
With five hillocks, perhaps haystacks gathered to one side.

I smile while trembling, one hundred twenty five pounds.
On a tiny juncture of bones,
muscles swaying as if a brisk breeze
tries to topple me.

I am *David,*
Quivering on ankles
While winds of time test my resolve.

Time to Forget

by Kaethe Kauffman

Six weeks is enough time to forget
My hybrid car needs gas,
(the tank empties on a six week schedule)
My hair isn't naturally brown
(the roots don't show for a month and a half)
I hate my enemies
(I'm a Pollyanna until forced into a showdown)

My face has scars
(I usually gaze in the mirror without glasses)
I'm shy,
(But compel myself to be brazen until I collapse)
I love sugar,
(And I don't indulge except for the occasional relapse)
I smoke,
(Ditto)

In a startled rush, I fill my gas tank, annoyed.
I dye my hair, disgruntled.
I tighten my spine, defensive.
I admit to a flawed face, humbled.
I submerge in solitude, relieved.
I eat cake, delighted.
I smoke sage, enlightened.

Sleeping with Strangers

by Kaethe Kauffman

I'm jealous of people who can sleep
In airplanes
In theaters
On park benches
At the beach

At the doctor's office
Surrounded by strangers.

The sleepers rest with mouths ajar,
Every muscle slack
In a happier world, grabbing bliss.

I practice in these places,
But can't surrender into oblivion
Unless helped by a small blue pill,
Cheating,
Woozy from strange chemicals.
I give up medication
And enviously watch others in their sweet dozes.

While seated in public spaces near random sleepers,
All races and ages,
I strive to share their purity.
They seem to dwell in the utter peace
I crave.

Mammoth

by Kaethe Kauffman

In a vast watery expanse, sun and sparkles bring joy to my squinting eyes.

Kindred

I paddle a small kayak, leaving a brilliant trail.

All at once, the glitter in front of me sways and moves in wide undulating arcs,
As if the water has come alive.
I jerk back, startled.
My eyes riveted on a large curved shape,
I slowly recognize as a monstrous back with bumpy rhythmic bones running lengthwise.
No teeth, no mouth appears,
Just a wide brown-grey moonscape covered with knobs, pits and scars.
I under stand wounds and admire the achievement they display.

The creature hovers by my side, passive,
Head lowered underwater.
After an hour it seems protective.
The most I can ask of any being is to stay close.

Entering the giant's territory,
I lower one hand into the water,
Fingers vulnerable in a slow drift,
A tender request for trust. I can almost touch my new friend.
The mammoth stays near my flimsy vessel, escorting me.

I read tiny lines and designs on its back like ancient writing
Suggesting the best course I should follow through the waters.
The behemoth remains steadfast beside me.

Irtika Kazi is a poet from Pune, India. Her poems, "A Call from the Alpines" was published in YuGen literary magazine in July 2017. Some of her poems have been selected to be published in The Indian Literature Magazine of Sahitya Akademi. Her poems were published in The Metaworker, an online literary magazine for millennials in March 2018. Her poem, "A hope to bloom" was featured in Duane Vorhees's poetry blog. Some poems were exhibited in the Museum of Goa for a poetry exhibit. "A Call from the Alpines" and "A hope to bloom" were published in the Brown Girl magazine of Houston, Texas in September 2017. Some of her poems were published on Spillwords Press. Further to that, her poem "Sunrise" was published in the anthology Fragrance of Asia, an Anthology by Asian poets, in January 2018. Another poem was published in the Contemporary Literary Review India journal in February 2018. Her work has been published in The Literary Hatchet print magazine in April 2018. She has performed her poems in open mics and events like The Pune heritage festival 2018, Women Writer's Fest by Shethepeople.
Link of the interview -
http://www.thesuccessmagazine.co.in/2018/02/reading-is-essential-practice-interview-irtikakazi.html?showComment=1519797648077#c8202478105051341627
Instagram – irtika.kazi
Email – irtika.kazi@gmail.com

The Tale of Sulasa's Courage: A mythological poem

by Irtika Kazi

The tale unfolds on the soil of *Benares*, shall I say,
Whence King *Brahmadatta* o'er the land held sway.
There lived a beautiful courtesan named *Sulasa*,
Emerged at once from the tales of *Jataka*.

Sulasa, for her beauty and immense wealth,
Was known by one and all there, who dwell'th.
On the same soil lived a barbarous thief,
As mighty as an elephant, as wretched as grief.

Named he was *Sattuka*, O' what a name!
To loot and plunder was his only aim.
For once he was trapped and caught by the King's men,
Who dragged and pulled him through the streets to kill, every now and then.

Whence *Sulasa's* eyes lay on this cowardly man,
She saw him with bound hands surrounded by the clan.
At once she decided to save him from them all,
For the flash of love and compassion did on her befall.

She traded thousand pieces with the killer for her Love to be freed,
And married him to live a life full of happiness and good deeds.

O', she was foolish to have trusted a thief like him,
For, he again revealed his stealthy nature and whim.

He was determined to rob *Sulasa* of her jewels,
So bade he her to offer them to the deity of the hills.
Sulasa, with her husband, went uphill to the deity,
There he revealed his true colors out of spontaneity.

He threatened *Sulasa* to undo her jewelry lest she be dead,
Sulasa was wise; she was in wisdom of him ahead.
She pled *Sattuka* to accept her dutiful obeisance,
And asked for his final embrace of complacence.

On his assent respectfully she encircled him thrice,
With power like a goddess, pushed him off the precipice.
Down went the wretched thief, her husband he were,
He died a painful death that went unnoticed and was blur.

Perceiving this act of courage,
The deity of the hill praised:
"Wisdom at times is not confined to men
A woman can chew wisdom now and then.

"Wisdom at times is not confined to men
Women are quick in counsel now and then."

How quick and keen she was the way to know,
She slew him like a deer with a full-stretched bow.

Beware you wrongdoers of Humanity!

Make these lines sacred for your own sanity.

"He that to great occasion fails to rise,
Falls, like that dull thief from the precipice."

Let us imbibe *Sulasa's* bravery, dear Women,
Let us engrave *Sulasa's* courage in us, dear Women,
In times of wrath, injustice and pain,
Let us wreak havoc on evil, like rain!

The Odyssey

by Irtika Kazi

Traveling through a deserted Land
Heaven knows where I'd be
Far off on the stretch of Sand
Looming Pyramids I see.
I see yonder the menacing Pharaoh, and the pompous Queen
Is this a figment of my imagination or a wakeful dream?
The scorching Sun cripples
My vision beyond the horizon,
The warm Wind blows in gusts
And my Odyssey wizens.
The Pharaoh, with his sturdy gait and more a stoic face
Is followed by his courtiers and men of noble race.

"Glory to our virtuous King! Glory unto thee!
The Gods and the Angels above, all bow down to thee."

"All bow down to me! Good Vizier[1], is' t true what you say?
Thou art the Holy power, Thou never go astray!"

The *Vizier* chuckled, "Aye! My King 'Tis true what we say.'"

I saw the Pharaoh pondering upon his million quests,
The battles he had fought and won with vigor and zest.
A sudden look of remorse came upon his sculpted profile,

The minister implored, "What is it that vexed my King?"
Walking down the aisle.
At last, He adjured one and all to follow him to the Nile.
The Pharaoh with his hand held high
Pointed at the sunlit sky
"By *Nut*[2]! It is indeed what a pleasant night!"
The people in a flash confessed,
"Indeed! What a pleasant night!"
For yet one more time, bade he the Priest
To jump into the Nile.
"O Priest! I am your God, so did you speak of me,
Jump for your God in the brine!"

The Priest neither stirred,
Nor for the fear of his Life obeyed his command.
Down went the seal from the Pharaoh's finger,
Down went the Crown grand.
Thereon forbade he the People

Not to submit to human clay,
But to worship that,
Which the Sun and earth obey.

My weary legs have stopped here
In the sight of a huge visage,
A half shattered Sphynx with a stoic and a menacing look
My visions turning out to be a mirage!

[1]Vizier–Wazir, Prime minister of the king's court
[2]Nut–Goddess of Sky, in Egyptian mythology.

Silence
by Irtika Kazi

Silence is Golden
It truly is,
For the people who can fathom
The Unspoken, the Unsaid.
Silence is the Virtue
Of people god-fearing,
For, the Devil lets loose tongues,
Of the Cunning and the Unnerving.
In times of Wrath and Injustice,
When the Evil wreaks havoc,

Seek Patience and Perseverance
And wait for Justice round the clock.
The World is an illusion
The inhabitants misleading
So what difference does it make?
In dissembling and deceiving.
Words of Wisdom, Words of Lore
Aid Humankind in survival galore
When still Ungodliness expands to Horror,
Replace good Silence with a thumping roar.

Silence is Noble,
Ah! As noble as Faith

Silence is Treacherous,
Alas! Enwrapped in hapless Swathe.

O' chatterer! Stop your un-mindful chatter
Seek guidance from the Mind and let go of the clatter
Forget not what shall remain past Humankind's shatter,
Silence--the solitary Truth shall matter.

A former interpreter, **Ihar Kazak**, switched to the pen (read computer) to come forth with some rare literature gems from Russian and Belarusian (cf worldcat.com Library of Congress, etc). His poetry has appeared internationally in various literary magazines.This is his second appearance on the Savant stage.

Notable prose contributions include:
THE TALES OF OLEG by Ihar Kazak (Createspace 2016)

INTERPRETER, TRANSLATE! THE TRAGIC COMEDY OF AN INTERPRETER (Beyond the Barrier 2006)

A FRIENDLY LETTER TO LENIN, NINOCHKA, AND OTHER STORIES by Igor Gregory Kozak (Edwin Mellen 2010)

Notable translations include:
THE LIQUIDATOR'S WIFE: A POST-CHERNOBYL TALE AND OTHER STORIES by Leanid Levanovich, Ihar Kazak and Aleksey Rahulya (Edwin Mellen 2015)

BITTER WORMWOOD WIND by Leanid Levanovich and Ihar Kazak (Edwin Mellen 2016)

A Poet So Rare

by Ihar Kazak

His verse is so diverse
his admirers are apt to exclaim.

He'll write about non-healing scars
of our national economy.

Then he'll make his 180 degree turn to
create the image of amorous exploits

Of lovers and their quivering
thighs and delighted sighs.

His topics may be the diminishing
rain forests and melting polar ice.

Or flowers in the meadows
polluted by toxic fumes of civilization.

Or starvation and wars
and social strife exacerbated

by Man's insipid inhumanity
and fiendish policies of state.

He even might find some humor
in life's decanter of noxious potions

in the struggle to exist and to
compete, destroy, and start

the vicious cycle once again.
He is a rarity,

for poets of today
are wearing pink glasses

of omission, neglect, and denigration.
They're living in a land of fantasy

While brutal reality is overwhelming
this, our frail world.

Nero's playing the fiddle, while Rome…

An Elixir of Vitality

by Ihar Kazak

Nay, we do not have in mind
That sexual potency pill
Which scientists say will make you blind.
Nay, this one's of a diff'rent kind.
It'll make your morn'

And your persona too
More bushy-tailed and newly-born:
This vim-vitality drink or two.
We're not proposing drugs or such
Nor even toxic medicine to take,
It'll surely make you want so-o much,
That it'll doubtlessly keep you awake...
We're talking coffee, no less nor more.
This morning elixir so vital for vitality,
Consumed by our millions galore:
Sometimes with sugar, cream, in solidarity.
With coffee lover numbers growing evermore;
They trust this liquid for its verity
Offering their praise, ignoring its lore.
Just think about its origins involving toil
Of many slave-like, coolie harvesters:
In baking sun with bending backs and human toll.
A lucrative deal for venal investors,
With coffee beans roasted and ground
By local, young and minimum-wage slaves.
Where else can this dubious pleasure be found
For four bucks of sipping and getting raves?
Oh, yes, it's coffee-time you're told:
Sounds of hissing, gurgling, and aroma bold.
Aye, life's simple pleasures are complex
When we are looking at the core of matters
One only soon becomes perplexed
When one's ideals are all in tatters.
Be heedless, hedonistic, and carefree!
And you'll just resort to life
As swinging primate in a tree

Shikeb Siddiqi has been writing articles and short stories for some time.

Missed My Stop
by Shikeb Siddiqi

Standing on the tracks I checked the horizon
The start of a new day would soon be arising
I squinted and frowned to harken the sun
The day was beginning but was already done

Staring at the ground I caught sight of my boots
Amidst the pebbles and the overgrown roots
My shoes were worn but not out of place
The glint from the rails reflecting my face

Every day I wait for the train to arrive
Is this a dream? Am I dead or alive?
An eternity I pondered without any haste
Perhaps I'm destined to never leave this place

The sun starts setting and I look to the sky
Another day ending filled with a lie
The light and the dark filled with a riddle
What of the grey inhabiting the middle
The next day I stood in the same position
As twilight approached I beheld a vision
A light was approaching with a rumbling sound
Shaking the earth and upsetting the ground

My heart was skipping at a resounding beat
I felt the existence of what I seek

Closer and nearer I felt the thunder
Here it came behold its wonder!

I watch as it passed and never slowed down
My shoulders were slumped as I look to the ground
Was it ever real or just a fleeting thought?
Love is something that should never be sought

Love is a betrayal that I have undoubtedly felt
As this emotion is based simply on wealth
It only exist in the realm of a dream
Where a train doesn't pass you with a full head of steam

Mirage

by Shikeb Siddiqi

What do I see in the far off distance?
Pushing me forward to ignore the resistance
To give up and fail and accept my fate
It's all that remains of my current state

A beleaguered individual without any hope
To give up the struggle and let go of the rope
Letting my soul tumble down the well
Leaving my expectations where they fell

Kindred

I stand in the Desert my breathing is slow
The sun beats down on me I can barely go
Hunched over with my hands on my knees
As the dust swirls around me and makes me wheeze

Coughing and choking on the blowing sand
My legs start buckling and I can barely stand
My will remains strong despite my belief
That inevitable failure will bring me relief

Heading towards gratification is the unconscious emotion
Sideways I move away from that notion
No happiness to be found in a desired vision
To reject its false promise is the best decision

Love is but a falsity that we ache to believe
The weight of this burden we must relieve
A waking dream that you choose to bear
Forget the promise for it doesn't care

Love makes our senses rise and float
Making us believe that our heart can hope
Don't be fooled by the mirage you perceive
For caring and affection you will not receive

T.W.Behz -- twenty-three years old from London -- Material Sciences PhD student at the University of Warwick.

Notable prose contributions include:
THE ESOTERIC MANUSCRIPT by T. W. Behz (T. W. Behz, 2017)

IGNORANCE IS BLISS

by T. W. Behz

Go back to days of bliss
The ignorance and its box of tricks
Its illusions grandiose and great
Gone by the time one learns to blink
Growing and growing by choice or otherwise
As one grows, because the bliss will shrink
Bliss and the ignorance hand in hand
The child uses to make a beautiful world brick by brick

My eyes open more than the average
Heat covers the view
The sun doesn't rise,
The ocean drowns it
The rain withheld by the cloud
From the thirsty planet
Roots dry
The bees have left the flower alone

Ignorance is bliss
And bliss bring ignorance
Such shame
Human feels obligated to be enlightened
If this is enlightenment
I do not want it

Music

by T. W. Behz

Fingers on the white and black keys
The composition was breathable.
Rare and charming

The melody tastes and smells very familiar
No doubt

Eighty-eight keys
Gentle pressure

The beauty comes from the brutality of the instrument
The sound comes from string's pain
Being hit by the hammer

Great representation of life

Thomas Koron was born in Grand Rapids, Michigan on May 19, 1977. He has attended Grand Rapids Community College, Aquinas College, Western Michigan University and the American Conservatory of Music. He remains active in Grand Rapids as a composer and performer.

Notable poetic contributions include:
"Black Satin/Snapdragon/The Veil of Night" in BELLWETHER MESSAGES: 2013Savant Poetry Anthology, Daniel S. Janik (ed)

"The Fading Scent of Perfume/The Days of Old/Autumn's Embers/Unforgiving Winter/He Rides Above the Clouds" in RUNNING FROM THE PACK: 2015/16 Savant Poetry Anthology, Helen R. Davis (ed)

"Lament Of The Banshee/Shining Eyes In The Dark/Fireflies/On This Bed Of Roses" in SHADOW AND LIGHT: 2017 Savant Poetry Anthology, Helen R. Davis (ed)

BEHOLD THE SWEET ANGEL

by Thomas Koron

Behold the sweet angel as she dances,
Bringing heaven with her into the night,
Her eyes glisten–spellbound with her glances–
That soft image twinkling in my sight.
And all her beauty is there on display,
Carrying the scent of every flower.
She breathes a fresh essence into the day;
My thoughts turn towards her at every hour.
Every time that I look up to the skies–
Recalling each moment shared in our youth.
She bore the gifts of heaven in her eyes;
If only courage had allowed my truth.
  When love exists–as we knew from the start–
  We must keep it safe, chained within the heart.

Multi-award-winning poet **Uhene** (Robert Maika'i Jr) lives in the beautiful Hawaii. Single, no children, he loves people and anything that tastes of mango. His Grandfather, Kawika Smith from Molokai, took him to his first theater movie at five years of age, a Samurai production, and thus began his poetic career on the streets of Waikiki.

Uhene's poems appear in:
BELLWETHER MESSAGES: 2013 Savant Poetry Anthology, Daniel S. Janik (ed)

RUNNING FROM THE PACK: 2015/16 Savant Poetry Anthology, Helen R. Davis (ed)

SHADOW AND LIGHT: 2107 Savant Poetry Anthology, Helen R. Davis (ed)

Dedicated to my mother Loretta (Pacada) Maika'i, my treasure, cherished gift from God. Much love and blessings Mom.

Elohim

by Uhene

Elohim, oh, Elohim,
Who was and is always,
Name of the Majestic One
Brought to life so all could truly exist.
Elohim, my Elohim,
May I kneel before Your Presence,
Giving to you my full
Reverence
And
Honor
That You rightly deserve.
Elohim, Oh Elohim, my Elohim,
You have come sacrificially, unselfishly into our
No, Your
World
Giving all you have in Glory.
Just so I may have the opportunity to breed
So shall prosper who love Thee continually and
unconditionally
Oh Elohim, my Elohim
Thank you for coming to dwell in the eternal present,
Presently among us all
Who with unconditional Love
As do completely believe in the Name above all names, Jesus
the Anointed.

Ken Rasti, also known as "Yes" among friends, is a Professor at several universities and a business management consultant for multiple organizations. An award-winning poet, he recently was inducted into the Heroes of Humanity Hall of Fame in recognition of his many positive community contributions. He lives in Hawaii, and has a daughter and a son who live and work in California.

Notable poetic contributions include:
"Aloha, I Love You: We Are All Connected" in BELLWETHER MESSAGES 2013 Savant Poetry Anthology, Daniel S. Janik (ed)
"Deeper than the Sea," "Sailing," "Sweet Moon," "Nature's Ecstasy" and "Dolphins" in SHADOW AND LIGHT 2017 Savant Poetry Anthology

Notable prose works include:
"Aloha, I Love You, We Are All Connected" in MESSAGES OF PEACE Words of Inspiration for Everyday Living from Hawaii (The Inspired Wellness Series Volume 1) by Worth Grace and Lori Chaffin (Inspired Wellness Publishing 2013)

Life is a Love Story

by Ken Rats

I need you
Do you need me?
My weary troubled heart needs you
My needs become doorways to my intimacy with you

I love you
An everlasting love
My love flows out from the center of eternity
My love knows no limits, no conditions

I want to see your face in every face
Let me immerse myself in your everlasting grace

I thought of you and golden flowers started to bloom
Distant dreams wondrously untangled
I heard a voice in my heart softly echoed …

Oh, your love is amazingly gentle
Your love leads me to precious discoveries
Peace, joy, tender intimacies
Distant dreams seem precariously close

All I have missed I will find in you
Every color in the sunset
Every glean in the water
Every soul that smiles

Every beautiful flower

I want to rest in you
Quiet in your love
Joyful in your beauty

When I am weary
I still feel your everlasting arms
My soul's lover
My soul's friend
My soul's pinnacle

Every evening in my dreams
I search for you like a hidden treasure
Every morning when I wake up
I find you
I love you Ke Akua
Life with you is a love story

Derek Bickerton (d. 2018) was a multi-award-winning English-born American linguist and academic who was Professor Emeritus at the University of Hawaii in Manoa. He is the author of numerous academic works as well as the renowned novelist of the Commandment Trilogy. A poet extraordinaire, he wrote extensively on the richness of life and the mysteries of death. He is survived by his wife, Yvonne.

Notable contributions include:
PAYROLL by Derek Bickerton (Eyre & Spottiswoode 1959)

THE GOLD RUN by Derek Bickerton (Eyre & Spottiswoode 1960)

THE MURDERS OF BOYSIE SINGH: Robber, Arsonist, Pirate, Mass Murderer, Vice, and Gambling King of Trinidad by Derek Bickerton (Arthur Barker 1962)

KING OF THE SEA: A Novel About a Man in the World of the Dolphins by Derek Bickerton (Random House 1979)

LANGUAGE AND SPECIES by Derek Bickerton (Univ of Chicago 1992)

LANGUAGE AND HUMAN BEHAVIOR (Jessie & John Danz Lectures) by Derek Bickerton (Univ of Washington1996)

THE DYNAMICS OF A CREOLE SYSTEM by Derek Bickerton (Cambridge Univ 2009)

BASTARD TONGUES: A Trailblazing Linguist Finds Clues to Our Common Humanity in the World's Lowliest Languages by Derek Bickerton (Hill and Wang 2009)

ADAM'S TONGUE: How Humans Made Language, How Language Made Humans by Derek Bickerton (Hill and Wang 2010)

THE DESERT AND THE CITY: Part 1 of the Commandment Trilogy by Derek Bickerton (Aignos 2013)

25 POEMS ON DEATH AND LOVE by Derek Bickerton (Createspace 2014)

MORE THAN NATURE NEEDS: Language, Mind, and Evolution by Derek Bickerton (Harvard Univ 2014)

IN THE HEART OF THE COUNTRY: Part 2 of the Commandment Trilogy by Derek Bickerton (Aignos 2015)

THE ROOTS OF LANGUAGE (Classics in Linguistics Vol 3) by Derek Bickerton (Language Science Press 2016)

What River and What Sea?

by Derek Bickerton

"into what river and what sea does your garden drain?" -
Question 597, Collins-Longman Study Atlas, © 1970

Clip clip the shears, and click! the secateurs
Prune the rank, sappy growth from the trim stem.
What won't burn can be stacked in a neat heap.
Clear the drains, scrape the gutters, tidy them,
Recalling a comforting saying of Voltaire's
As the light fades. Haven't we earned our sleep?

All night it rains. Water whelms the world.
Withered clippings ride on the gutter current.
Did we leave anything out to be washed away?
No. By our bright light you can see the torrent
Pouring harmlessly off into the wild --
Our well-kept portion will be dry by day.

Who knows where it swells through lands of drought and drowning,
Of hollow laws, casual injustices?
Plump your pillow, put out your light and accept
That we all did our part, that we can't be expected to guess
Into what river and what sea, by morning,
Beasts, houses, bloated children will be swept.

A Limited Number Of Mornings

by Derek Bickerton

For a limited number of mornings
I'll wake, turn, take you in my arms and return,
(Holding you) back into the dream I've been dreaming,
Into a sleep, ah! sweeter and deeper by far than any
Ever before known --
For a limited number of mornings

Knowing one day it will happen
That I'll wake, turn, take you in my arms, and find
The life I loved more than my own, the sweet warmth of you,
Flown like a soft secret moth from the shards of your being.

Or I'll wake, turn, reach out and touch...nothing
(Fooled by the dream I've been dreaming into believing
You were there still, happy as ever) -- bearing
Again the unbearable horror of your loss
For a limited number of mornings.

Or I won't wake, turn, or take you, but remain
In a sleep deeper (not sweeter) by far than any
Ever before know --
This for me the easier and the worse
Leaving for you the unbearable horror of loss
For a limited number of mournings.

Envoi

by Derek Bickerton

Don't expect any more,
No, not even one.
Having sung his songs, the swan
Awaits his cue to exit.

I took life in both hands
Trying to squeeze it dry.
Now it's a husk. To try
Letting go won't be easy.

As the gates of each sense
One after another close
And the creek's current flows
Every week shallower

Trying to retain
Some shreds of dignity
Will be enough for me...

The fuck with singing.

First Breath - 2010 Savant Anthology of Poems
Zachary M. Oliver (Editor)
72 pp. 5.25" x 8" Softcover
ISBN 978-0-9845552-2-2

Twenty-nine poems by ten outstanding poets and writers selected for their outstanding merit, including Helen Doan, Erin L. George, Jack Howard, Daniel S. Janik, Scott Mastro, Zachary M. Oliver, Francis H. Powell, Gabjirel Ra, V. Bright Saigal and Orest Stocco.

Wavelengths - 2011 Savant Poetry Anthology
Zachary M. Oliver (Editor)
102 pp. 5.25" x 8" Softcover
ISBN 978-0-9829987-6-2

Thirty-eight poems by sixteen outstanding poets and writers including Four Arrows, Penny Lynn Cates, J. R. Coleman, Nadia Cox, Helen Doan, Erin L George, IKO, Daniel S. Janik, Vivekanand Jha, A. K. Kelly, Zachary M. Oliver, Cara Richardson, Michael Shorb, Jason Sturner, Jean Yamasaki Toyama and Jeremy Ussher.

LONDON BOOK FESTIVAL AWARD

Fifty-Eight Stones - 2012 Savant Poetry Anthology

Daniel S. Janik (Editor)

128 pp. 5.25" x 8" Softcover

ISBN 978-0-9852506-5-2

Thirty-four outstanding poems by eleven exceptional and many award-winning poets including Shawn Canon, Nadia Cox, Helen Doan, David Gemmell, Richard Hookway, Daniel S. Janik, Vivekanand Jha, Doc Krinberg, Julie McKinney, Francis Powell and Jean Yamasaki Toyama.

Bellwether Messages - 2013 Savant Poetry Anthology

Daniel S. Janik (Editor)

134 pp. 5.25" x 8" Softcover Pocketbook

ISBN 978-0-9886640-4-3

Thirty-two selected poems by fourteen outstanding poets including Tender Bastard, Shawn P. Canon, Natascha Hoover, IKO, Daniel S. Janik, Vivekanand Jha, Thomas Koron, Doc Krinberg, Cathal Patrick Little, Peter Mallett, Emma Myles, Ken Rasti, Uhene' and Ashley Vaughan.

LONDON BOOK FESTIVAL AWARD

Edited by Suzanne Langford

Volutions - 2014 Savant Poetry Anthology
Suzanne Langford (Editor)
146 pp. 5.25" x 8" Softcover Pocketbook
ISBN 978-0-9915622-1-3

Thirty-six exceptional poems by fourteen outstanding poets including Noemi Villagrana Barragan, Elsha Bohnert, Hans Brinckmann, Helen R. Davis, K. Lauren de Boer, Duandino, Lonner F. Holden, Daniel S. Janik, Kaethe Kauffman, Suzanne Langford, Lucretia Leong, C. P. Little, Leilani Madison and Lady Mariposa.

LA, LONDON, PARIS and PACFIC RIM BOOK FESTIVAL AWARDS

Running from the Pack - 2015/16 Savant Poetry Anthology

Helen R. Davis (Editor)
100 pp. 5.25" x 8" Softcover
ISBN 978-0-9963255-5-4

Thirty-five selected poems by fifteen outstanding poets including Dylan DiMarchi, Teuta S. Rizaj, Uhene, Marianne Smith, Danny Smith, Manal Hamad, Thomas Koron, J. Okajima, A. G. Hayes, Kelsea Kennedy, C. P. Little, Helen R. Davis, Doc Krinberg, Kaethe Kauffman and Daniel S. Janik.

PACFIC RIM BOOK FESTIVAL AWARD

Shadow and Light - 2017 Savant Poetry Anthology

Edited by Helen R. Davis

134 pp. 5.25" x 8" Softcover Pocketbook

ISBN 978-0-9972472-8-2

Sixty-four selected poems by twenty-two outstanding poets including, in order of appearance, Rose Seaquill, Bipul Banerjee, Dr. Mike, Doc Krinberg, Jock Armour, Mr. Ben, Emily Anderson, Marianne Smith, Carolina Casas, Cigeng Zhang, Thomas Koron, Mark Daniel Seiler, Dwight Armbrust Jr, Uhene, Daniel S. Janik, Lonner F. Holden, Sara Hawley, Ihar Kazak, Barbara Bailey, V. Bright Saigal, Ken Rasti and Teuta S. Rizaj.

If you enjoyed ***Shadow and Light****, consider these other fine poetic works from Savant Books and Publications:*

Savant Poetry Anthologies

First Breath (2010) edited by Z. M. Oliver
Wavelengths (2011) edited by Zachary M. Oliver
Fifty-Eight Stones (2012) edited by Daniel S. Janik
Bellwether Messages (2013) edited by Daniel S. Janik
Volutions (2014) edited by Suzanne Langford
Running from the Pack (2015/16) edited by Helen R. Davis
Shadow and Light (2017) edited by Helen R. Davis

Savant Poetry Collections

Footprints, Smiles and Little White Lies by Daniel S. Janik
The Illustrated Middle Earth by Daniel S. Janik
Last and Final Harvest by Daniel S. Janik

Aignos Poetry Collections

Iwana by Alvaro Leiva
Prepositions by Jean Yamasaki Toyama

...as well as these other fine books from Savant Books and Publications:

Essay, Essay, Essay by Yasuo Kobachi
Aloha from Coffee Island by Walter Miyanari
Footprints, Smiles and Little White Lies by Daniel S. Janik
The Illustrated Middle Earth by Daniel S. Janik
Last and Final Harvest by Daniel S. Janik
A Whale's Tale by Daniel S. Janik
Tropic of California by R. Page Kaufman
Tropic of California (the companion music CD) by R. Page Kaufman
The Village Curtain by Tony Tame
Dare to Love in Oz by William Maltese
The Interzone by Tatsuyuki Kobayashi
Today I Am a Man by Larry Rodness
The Bahrain Conspiracy by Bentley Gates
Called Home by Gloria Schumann
Kanaka Blues by Mike Farris
First Breath edited by Z. M. Oliver
Poor Rich by Jean Blasiar
The Jumper Chronicles by W. C. Peever
William Maltese's Flicker by William Maltese
My Unborn Child by Orest Stocco
Last Song of the Whales by Four Arrows
Perilous Panacea by Ronald Klueh
Falling but Fulfilled by Zachary M. Oliver
Mythical Voyage by Robin Ymer
Hello, Norma Jean by Sue Dolleris
Richer by Jean Blasiar
Manifest Intent by Mike Farris
Charlie No Face by David B. Seaburn
Number One Bestseller by Brian Morley
My Two Wives and Three Husbands by S. Stanley Gordon
In Dire Straits by Jim Currie
Wretched Land by Mila Komarnisky
Chan Kim by Ilan Herman
Who's Killing All the Lawyers? by A. G. Hayes

Ammon's Horn by G. Amati
Wavelengths edited by Zachary M. Oliver
Almost Paradise by Laurie Hanan
Communion by Jean Blasiar and Jonathan Marcantoni
The Oil Man by Leon Puissegur
Random Views of Asia from the Mid-Pacific by William E. Sharp
The Isla Vista Crucible by Reilly Ridgell
Blood Money by Scott Mastro
In the Himalayan Nights by Anoop Chandola
On My Behalf by Helen Doan
Traveler's Rest by Jonathan Marcantoni
Keys in the River by Tendai Mwanaka
Chimney Bluffs by David B. Seaburn
The Loons by Sue Dolleris
Light Surfer by David Allan Williams
The Judas List by A. G. Hayes
Path of the Templar—Book 2 of The Jumper Chronicles by W. C. Peever
The Desperate Cycle by Tony Tame
Shutterbug by Buz Sawyer
Blessed are the Peacekeepers by Tom Donnelly and Mike Munger
The Bellwether Messages edited by D. S. Janik
The Turtle Dances by Daniel S. Janik
The Lazarus Conspiracies by Richard Rose
Purple Haze by George B. Hudson
Imminent Danger by A. G. Hayes
Lullaby Moon (CD) by Malia Elliott of Leon & Malia
Volutions edited by Suzanne Langford
In the Eyes of the Son by Hans Brinckmann
The Hanging of Dr. Hanson by Bentley Gates
Flight of Destiny by Francis Powell
Elaine of Corbenic by Tima Z. Newman
Ballerina Birdies by Marina Yamamoto
More More Time by David B. Seabird
Crazy Like Me by Erin Lee
Cleopatra Unconquered by Helen R. Davis
Valedictory by Daniel Scott
The Chemical Factor by A. G. Hayes

Quantum Death by A. G. Hayes
Running from the Pack edited by Helen R. Davis
Big Heaven by Charlotte Hebert
Captain Riddle's Treasure by GV Rama Rao
All Things Await by Seth Clabough
Tsunami Libido by Cate Burns
Finding Kate by A. G. Hayes
The Adventures of Purple Head, Buddha Monkey and…by Erik Bracht
In the Shadows of My Mind by Andrew Massie
The Gumshoe by Richard Rose
Cereus by Z. Roux
Shadow and Light edited by Helen R. Davis
The Solar Triangle by A. G. Hayes
A Real Daughter by Lynne McKelvey
StoryTeller by Nicholas Bylotas
Bo Henry at Three Forks by Daniel D. Bradford
One Night in Bangkok by Keith R. Rees

Coming Soon:
Navel of the Sea by Elizabeth McKague

Savant Books and Publications
http://www.savantbooksandpublications.com

Kindred

...and these from our new imprint, Aignos Publishing:

The Dark Side of Sunshine by Paul Guzzo
Happy that it's Not True by Carlos Aleman
Cazadores de Libros Perdidos by German William Cabasssa Barber [Spanish]
The Desert and the City by Derek Bickerton
The Overnight Family Man by Paul Guzzo
There is No Cholera in Zimbabwe by Zachary M. Oliver
John Doe by Buz Sawyers
The Piano Tuner's Wife by Jean Yamasaki Toyama
Nuno by Carlos Aleman
An Aura of Greatness by Brendan P. Burns
Polonio Pass by Doc Krinberg
Iwana by Alvaro Leiva
University and King by Jeffrey Ryan Long
The Surreal Adventures of Dr. Mingus by Jesus Richard Felix Rodriguez
Letters by Buz Sawyers
In the Heart of the Country by Derek Bickerton
El Camino De Regreso by Maricruz Acuna [Spanish]
Diego in Two Places by Carlos Aleman
Prepositions by Jean Yamasaki Toyama
Deep Slumber of Dogs by Doc Krinberg
Saddam's Parrot by Jim Currie
Beneath Them by Natalie Roers
Chang the Magic Cat by A. G. Hayes
Illegal by E. M. Duesel
Island Wildlife: Exiles, Expats and Exotic Others by Robert Friedman
The Winter Spider by Doc Krinberg

Coming Soon:
The Princess in My Mind by J. G. Matheny

Aignos Publishing | an imprint of Savant Books and Publications
http://www.aignospublishing.com

TO BRI TURNER & OHANA

MAY THE LIGHT
REFLECT ALL THE BEAUTY
OF THE PATHWAY
FOLLOW MOST ALLURING
STEP UP TO THE
HEAVENS!

E PULE LANI Oé
PRAY FROM HEAVEN
TO YOU

UA FENE

Made in the USA
Monee, IL
02 April 2021

63435774R00066